KILLER ANIMALS
WOLVES
ON THE HUNT
REVISED EDITION

by Lori Polydoros

Reading Consultant:
Barbara J. Fox
Reading Specialist
North Carolina State University

Content Consultant:
Douglas W. Smith, Leader
Yellowstone Wolf Project
Yellowstone National Park, Wyoming

CAPSTONE PRESS
a capstone imprint

Blazers is published by Capstone Press,
1710 Roe Crest Drive, North Mankato, Minnesota, 56003
www.mycapstone.com

Library of Congress Cataloging-in-Publication Data is available on the Library of Congress website.
ISBN: 978-1-5157-6227-0 (revised paperback)
ISBN: 978-1-5157-6228-7 (ebook pdf)

Editorial Credits
Christine Peterson, editor; Kyle Grenz, set designer; Bobbi J. Wyss, book designer;
Svetlana Zhurkin, media researcher

Image Credits
Creatas: Cover, 5, 18-19; iStockphoto: John Pitcher, 24-25; Shutterstock: Al Parker, 22-23,
AndreAnita, 17, Bildagentur Zoonar GmbH, 10-11, David Osborn, 9, Jens Metschurat,
13, Pesat Jaroslav, 20-21, Ronnie Howard, 26, Tom Tietz, 28-29, Volt Collection, 6-7, Wim
Verhagen, 14-15

Printed and bound in the USA.
009969R

TABLE OF CONTENTS

POWERFUL HUNTERS

A wolf runs on top of a hill, looking for a meal. It spies a lone deer. The wolf sprints down toward its **prey**.

prey — an animal hunted by another animal for food

The deer stumbles through the snow. Other wolves from the **pack** bound forward. They attack the deer with powerful bites. The deer soon dies. The wolves tear into their feast.

pack — a family of animals

KILLER FACT

Wolves usually eat about 10 pounds
(5 kilograms) of meat a day.

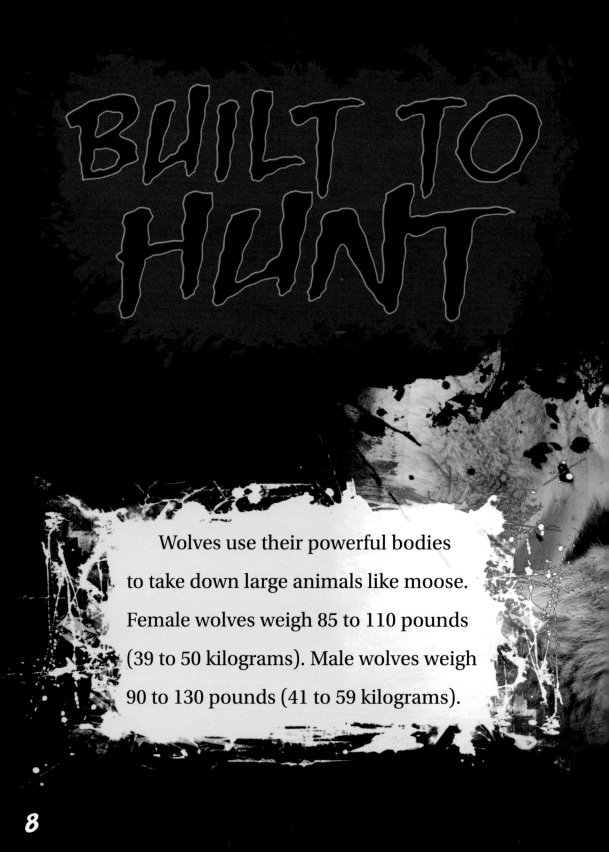

BUILT TO HUNT

Wolves use their powerful bodies to take down large animals like moose. Female wolves weigh 85 to 110 pounds (39 to 50 kilograms). Male wolves weigh 90 to 130 pounds (41 to 59 kilograms).

With a burst of speed, wolves go in for the kill. Wolves can run as fast as 38 miles (61 kilometers) per hour. They may roam 10 to 30 miles (16 to 48 kilometers) a day to track prey.

KILLER FACT

Wolves have big feet that act like snowshoes.
Their feet don't sink into deep snow.

Wolves attack prey with 42 sharp teeth. Four sharp **canine** teeth grab and tear prey. Their back teeth crush bones and grind meat. Wolves use their small front teeth to pull skin off of their kill.

KILLER FACT

Wolves usually bite the nose or back end of their prey.

canine — a long, pointed tooth

Sharp **senses** make wolves expert trackers. Wolves smell prey from more than 1 mile (1.6 kilometers) away. Their sense of smell is 100 times stronger than humans.

sense — a way of knowing about your surroundings

PACK ATTACK

Wolves live and hunt in packs of five to 10 animals. Wolves openly hunt their prey. Sometimes wolves watch prey from behind trees and brush.

KILLER FACT

Wolves find it easier to make a kill in winter when animals are weak.

KILLER FACT

To save energy, wolves follow the same trails as their prey.

Wolves race toward their prey. The prey runs and tries to escape. But wolves are **swift** hunters. In a matter of minutes, the wolves catch and kill their prey.

swift — happening or done quickly

Wolves usually attack sick, old, or very young animals. Wolves use their strong jaws to overpower the weak animals. Their bites can crack open the leg bone of a large animal.

KILLER FACT

Sometimes the pack cannot eat the entire kill. Wolves bury leftover food to eat later.

Wolf Diagram

thick coat

tail

ear

sharp teeth

wide paws

WILD WOLVES

Wolves help keep the **ecosystem** in balance. Wolves hunt animals that eat plants. Without wolves, these animals would eat too many plants. Then other animals would not have enough food and could starve.

ecosystem — a group of animals and plants that work together with their surroundings

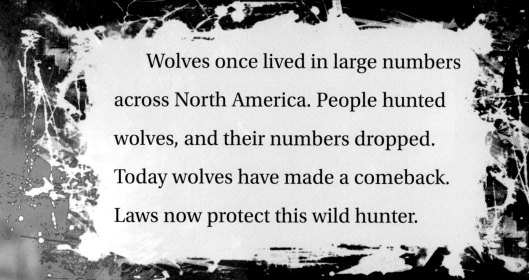

Wolves once lived in large numbers across North America. People hunted wolves, and their numbers dropped. Today wolves have made a comeback. Laws now protect this wild hunter.

KILLER FACT

Most wolves live in North America, Europe, and Asia.

Wild Bite!

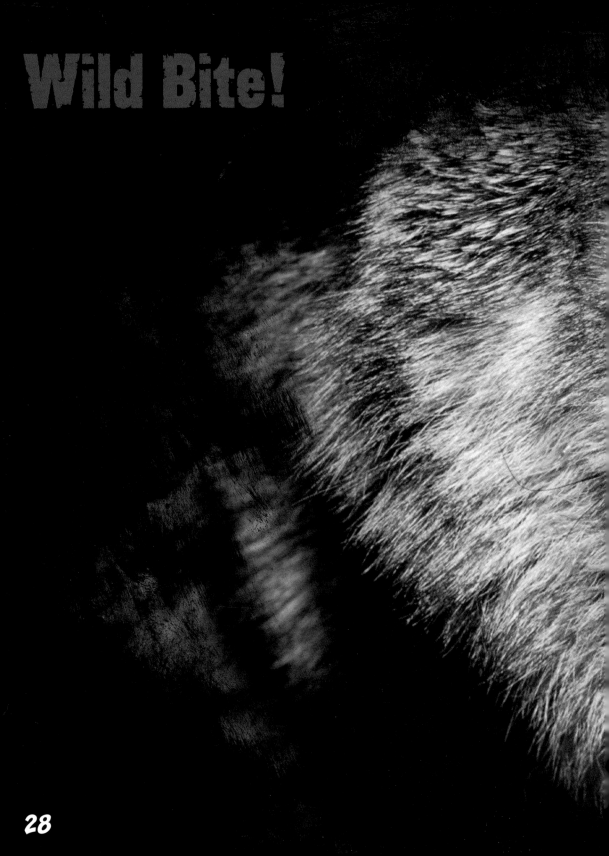

GLOSSARY

canine (KAY-nyn) — a long, pointed tooth

ecosystem (EE-koh-sis-tuhm) — a group of animals and plants that work together with their surroundings

pack (PAK) — a family of animals that lives in the same environment and travels together; wolves travel together in a pack.

prey (PRAY) — an animal hunted by another animal for food

sense (SENSS) — a way of knowing about your surroundings; hearing, smelling, touching, tasting, and seeing are the five senses.

swift (SWIFT) — happening or done quickly

READ MORE

Barnes, Julia. *The Secret Lives of Wolves.* The Secret Lives of Animals. Milwaukee: Gareth Stevens, 2007.

Bjorklund, Ruth. *Wolves.* Endangered! New York: Marshall Cavendish Benchmark, 2009.

Miller, Sara Swan. *Wolves.* Paws and Claws. New York: PowerKids Press, 2008.

INTERNET SITES

FactHound offers a safe, fun way to find Internet sites related to this book. All of the sites on FactHound have been researched by our staff.

Here's all you do:

Visit *www.facthound.com*

FactHound will fetch the best sites for you!

Index